The Life of a Youth

Series One

Why Are You Here?

Mobu Eberendu

KNOWING THE PERSON THAT MATTERS THE MOST

Copyright © 2018 by Mobughichi Eberendu

All rights reserved. This book or any portion thereof may not be reproduced or used in any manner whatsoever without the express written permission of the publisher except for the use of brief quotations in a book review.

Except otherwise referenced, all scriptural quotations were from the (KJV) King James Version or (NIV) New International Version.

All rights reserved other quotes throughout the book were put in bold or italics letters for Author emphasis with clear references.

Paperback ISBN: 9781718175006

Printed in United Kingdom

Delight waves publishing, 2018

DEDICATION PAGE

To everyone who is seeking to find a deeper understanding of who they are and why they have been placed on this earth by The Almighty God.

To the billions of people seeking to find their purpose. To the downtrodden, outcast, uneducated, and ill-treated youths across the world. This book is written to speak hope, give direction and bring light to all aspects of your life, especially in the discovery of your true identity.

To the Legacy of Dr Myles Munroe whose work continuously inspires various aspects of my life and causes me to take action even in my own little way.

To my future wife, unborn children, and grandchildren who I pray will be agents and teachers of positive change.

To my parents, Rev. L. E. Osisiogu and Mrs Judith Osisiogu who brought me up in the way of God and continuously pray for my progress.

To my younger sister, Olive N. Eberendu who continues to allow God to use her to empower and build the youths of her generation.

To all my friends who have inspired me and lived as exemplary youths by devoting themselves to worthy causes that protect, preserves, and advances human life.

To the source of all true gifts, the creator of destinies and sustainer of life.

May Your truth explode in the hearts of all who read the pages of this book.

ACKNOWLEDGEMENT

Almost all great things that humans have achieved came to be due to a collective effort. It is a great honour to have my name on the covers of this book, but what I do not take for granted are the efforts of my friends who acted as editors, designers and promoters. You all helped to make this dream a reality, may God bless you all.

CONTENTS

Author's Forward: Providing independence to people's barriers

1 **Who are the Youth?** 1
2 **Why are You here?** 4
3 **My Story** 21
4 **Some Keys that Helped Me Find Me** 43
5 **What is Purpose, Mission, and Vision?** ...64
6 **Components of Your Why** 71
7 **Conclusion** 75
8 **Oh, One More Thing** 81
9 **Summary** 83
10 **Another book by the Author** 87

AUTHOR'S FOREWORD

Providing Independence to People's Barriers

The gifts were present, but the contents were absent. I called upon God to reveal exactly why I was sent to earth and sustained by him despite all the attempts the devil made on my life even before birth. People who are close to me know that I have a beautiful sister, but what most do not know is that I was supposed to have two sisters and two brothers, but only one of my siblings made it. Out of all my siblings, medically, I was the one who they felt would not make it. Hence, I was named *Mobughichi*, which means *if not God*. Therefore, if God has preserved my life despite everything, it means that He must have a clearly defined *why* for me, and this was exactly what I went in desperate search of. Walking down to the Portsmouth University business school from The Hard train station, I heard God say to me clearly; *"you are born to provide independence to people's barriers"*, for a moment, I felt someone was physically speaking to me as I frantically looked around in search of the voice. It was a familiar voice however because it was not the first time I'd heard God speak to me.

After this experience, God started to unveil exactly what He meant over the years. One of the most important things He unveiled was that Man's biggest barrier is not external, but internal.

2 Corinthians 10:4-5 (NKJV) *"For the weapons of our warfare are not carnal but mighty in God for pulling down strongholds, casting down arguments and every high thing that exalts itself against the knowledge of God, bringing every thought into captivity to the obedience of Christ"*. A lot of people are fighting the wrong battles; the weapons of our warfare are for pulling down strongholds in our minds, and for shutting down barrier inducing thoughts that make us prisoners of our own selves. This is exactly what this book seeks to do. It will challenge some concepts that I believe have held young people back for decades, and help guide you to the paths of maximizing your true potential.

Who are the Youth

Your youth is one of the most important stages of your life on this earth as it provides the foundations for the rest of your life. If the foundations are corrupt or without substance, then the house (your life) has the possibility of crumbling. If the house is built on firm foundations then it will stand strong in the face of trials.

[24] "Therefore whoever hears these sayings of Mine, and does them, I will liken him to a wise man who built his house on the rock: [25] and the rain descended, the floods came, and the winds blew and beat on that house; and it did not fall, for it was founded on the rock.

[26] "But everyone who hears these sayings of Mine, and does not do them, will be like a foolish man who built his house on the sand: [27] and the rain descended, the floods came, and the winds blew and beat on that house; and it fell. And great was its fall."

Matthew 7: 24-27

It is important to determine who a youth is as this book is applicable to those people who are currently in that stage of their life; in between their childhood and fully understanding who they are and what they have been placed on this earth to do.

I must stress that this is irrespective of your age. A youthful stage of life is an important stage in life and must not be overlooked or undermined because this is a time that can either make or break you. So this book will give insight into many questions I have asked myself as a youth, which I also believe you might have asked yourself.

I have had many difficulties in answering a lot of these questions which is why more than 10 years has gone into my research on this topic. I started this book at the age of 13; it was my English presentation project at school. I have divided these questions into 8 specific groups, which as I have grown I have realised are respective books of their own. So, I will try my best to pass on this knowledge from my several years of learning and research on these very important topics which will be in the following series:

1. **Why are You here:** Knowing the person that matters the most
2. **Who is a Friend:** Distinguishing between a friend, a frenemy and an enemy
3. **What on earth is this Love thing:** Distinguishing between youthful infatuations and real love
4. **Should I do it:** Decisions and consequences
5. **What is Life all about:** Principles for earthly life and its significance to us
6. **Are they my Parents:** Distinguishing between discipline and abuse
7. **Who can help me:** God's help versus man's help
8. **Why is my life precious:** Defining the concept of value

Why are You Here

This will be no doubt the most important question you will need to answer. Everything in your life, every decision, every relationship, every knowledge you decide to acquire, every school and subject you study, every mentor you decide to follow, everyone you decide not to follow will be decided by this single question.

Why am I here? What is my purpose? Who am I? What makes me different from the rest? Am I different from the rest?

These are questions that I personally struggled with growing up, and from my conversations with a lot of young people I know this question (Why am I here?) is a leading culprit to a lot of worrying, depression, self-esteem issues, and a host of other issues that has cost the lives of many young people who got so fed up that some even opted to take their own lives because of the lack of a sense of meaning for their lives.

Reasons you must know your "why"

The world and your environment will try to subdue you

If you do not know what your why is (note: I do not exempt anyone from this category so this includes your parents, best friends, wives, teachers, media, girlfriends or boyfriends), literally everyone will try to subdue you. Remember when as a child you said "I will like to be ...." and immediately an adult or someone close to you said to you "be realistic", another way you can imagine what people are trying to communicate is, they're telling you to be normal, be average; the way I look at it, they're telling you to be mediocre. A wise man once said, *"An epidemic of mediocrity which has so cut across our society today has made those that do just a little bit more genius"*. Dr Myles Munroe

I must stress this, you do not need to be realistic with your vision, that is why it is your vision, do not expect everyone to agree or encourage your vision. I do not even expect you to fully comprehend your vision; some of it will definitely seem bigger or seemingly crazy to your understanding right now, but you will do yourself a great deal of favour to stay with it 'til the end no matter the pressures that might come. I can imagine how people laughed at Bill Gates (university dropout) when he said that he saw a future where every household had a computer, note this was at a time when some countries only had one computer. Imagine if he had stopped because of pressures from people and family. Imagine if Thomas Edison stopped pursuing his vision to invent the light bulb. He was sacked by the company he started the research for, left by his wife, and deemed insane just because of his vision to create the light bulb. Imagine if Obama did not believe because of the history of America, that America can have a black president. I can imagine a white child in Africa not believing he or she can ever aspire to be president in their country or a black man or woman in the UK not believing he or she can be prime minister. I can even imagine what my parents would say to me if I said to them I aspire to be the prime minister of the United Kingdom (I don't), but let's imagine I did, I can imagine the types of words my parents will use to describe my level of insanity, I can imagine the friends and teachers who would call me crazy. Listen, they don't matter. Your vision is personal to you and must guide you through life until it is fulfilled. Do not be arrogant about it, just humbly say thank you to your unbelievers, but remain dedicated to your vision and try not to spend a lot of time with these people (I do not mean you shouldn't spend time with your parents). Learn how to communicate your vision clearly; I am sure you will find people like me who are there to believe in you.

You will face a lot of challenges

I hope that broke your bubble. In life, challenges will come. However, people who succeeded like John Ford and like I will, are people who remain focused on their vision until they are successful.

F.O.C.U.S. "Follow One Course Until Successful"

No challenge you face today is greater than the difference your vision will make to mankind. Imagine the state the world would be in right now if we did not have cars. A man failed so many times and went bankrupt five times before the first car was produced. Imagine if he got fed up with his failures or periods of financial lack; perhaps we would still all have horse-drawn carriages who knows? It was this first breakthrough that made others dare to dream about the concept of buses or even flying. To see your vision fulfilled will not only affect your life; it will unlock a whole chain of people who will go on and fulfil several dreams and visions. You owe it to this world not to die with your vision; the cemeteries already have stolen a lot from us, which is why it is said to be the wealthiest place on earth. Don't add to it, be part of the movement of people who die empty. Do not die with that book, movie or song inside of you. Refuse for the cure to cancer to die, and be laid to rest in a cemetery whilst millions of lives are wasted every day. Do not die with that idea; do not let fear cause you to become a generational thief.

What we know as Dubai today was mostly desert a few years ago; imagine if someone died with such a vision. It is my conviction that everyone has a very important and time altering vision in them, but my prayer is that you as a reader will fulfil that vision and make that difference you were created to make.

"You Are That Solution That Is Sought After"

People will give you something to believe in if you don't have something already

This is already being done on every level possible starting with your family. Which is why I will recommend finding yourself very early in life (know the person that matters the most); this will separate you from the norm quite early in life. I am very confident of this fact; it will be the biggest favour you will do for yourself. I think I was about 5 years old when I started to discover some subtle differences in my persona and this self-portrait determined what my conduct has been.

"Your self-portrait will determine your self-conduct"

Having an insight into my future destiny protected me from a lot of costly mistakes. In areas I chose or was deceived to go against my inert self I paid dearly for it. This is why I do not want you to go through the same situation. It will save you from a lot of heartaches, wasted years, and wasted resources.

"Experience is not the best teacher; it is the worst teacher ever, learning from other peoples experience is a much more worthy course to follow and much less expensive" Dr Mike Murdock

"Do not park in the same parking lot your father's car packed-up"

Can you remember at home when as a child your parents said things that suggested you were the dummy in your house because you did not perform as good as your siblings in school; how you felt they had a favourite that was not you? Do you remember how you actually started feeling like a dummy? how they told you to be like one family friend or cousin? I have been in your situation. However, what helped to keep me going and still love my parents amongst other things, was and is still the fact that I identified I had a different existential *why* to the people I was being compared to. Just like you cannot compare your arms and your feet, no one should compare you to another individual because you are different. You need to understand this; I can't stress it enough. Even if you have similarities in purpose it does not matter. A quick example you might relate to; if I should ask, between Michael Jackson (MJ) and Jimi Hendrix who is better? I'm sure the first question that came to you if you know them was *at what?* Yes, they are both musicians, but they both excelled in different areas, MJ is a world great vocalist and dancer, whilst Mr Hendrix is believed to be a world-renowned guitarist.

"Notice I did not use greatest, this is because I believe in your future"

I remember even right from primary school when they divided us to classes A, B and C. The kids in classes A were believed to be the intelligent kids and people like me were always in classes B or C. Yes it hurt, but I did not let it define me. Whilst everyone might have looked at us as less intelligent, I chose to see myself as different. That is what knowing your why can do for you. It continued through secondary school, they kept up with this process of separation. It was painful sometimes, but it did not make me stop. To help myself keep believing, I started writing *I can do all things through Christ* on all my books. I was not even allowed to take the higher GCSE like most kids did in Maths and English. I was put on foundation level; for people who do not live in the UK, this means the most I could get was a C for these subjects. However, I was determined that this will not make any difference to my future.

I was determined to persevere until I fulfilled my purpose, I believed that nothing will stop me as long as I remain committed to fulfilling what I have been destined for.

Have you been told nothing good comes out of people from your country, state, county, city, estate, family or even your race? I know what it feels like to be in all of those situations. Don't you believe me? Ok take a trip down memory lane with me; I'm from Nigeria, predominantly known at the moment for several bad reasons. In Nigeria, I'm from Abia State, which is known at the moment as one of the poorest, unproductive and one of the dirtiest cities in the world. During my teens, I moved to the UK. I grew up in a place called Blacon in Chester in Cheshire County. This place was so small, but it was always topping the chart as one of the worst places to live in the UK, their crime levels were astonishing. I remember several kids like me who were entrenched in crime in my area; people comfortably walked up to me and asked if I wanted drugs. Although I did not live in a council estate, everybody in Chester took people from Blacon as council dwellers. I remember one day at a shop in the city centre, I was sent to do the shopping for the house, included in the list I was given was a beverage that needed an ID, I wasn't really aware at this point that I needed ID for this so when I went to pay, the shop assistant was so rude to me instead of telling me what I did wrong. I asked to speak to a manager and when this man came he was briefed by the shop assistant. He went directly to take my groceries away and asked me to leave the shop. I so felt humiliated, so I told him I will report how he treated me to my parents when I get home, he turned to me asking where home was. Before I could reply, he said: "I'm sure you are from Blacon". I was gobsmacked because I was not used to people openly using my location of residence against me, but I walked out saying to myself; "I might be from Blacon, but one day, I will have what it takes to buy your shop". Just in case you haven't realised yet I'm also black, and historically blacks have faced a lot of prejudice. So some people can say quite comfortably, what does this guy have going for him? I will always say to whoever cares to know; I know my *why*. When you discover your why, do not let anything act as an obstacle. If Obama never took the plunge to become the President in America, if he got caught up with the prejudice, he would have limited himself to the seemingly prestigious senate-house, but his vision went further and became a reality. Martin Luther King Jr dreamed of when blacks will be treated like whites, which got a few movements going. Even as great as he was I am sure he would have been seen as utterly mad if he said I dream of when a black man will be your president.

Dare to dream outside your confines; you are the only one who can stop yourself from fulfilling your dreams. Nothing is impossible to him that believes.

You will spend time on a Job rather than Working

Work is something you were made to do; your job is something you are paid to do. Work is something you are doing out of belief in your vision, you never retire from your work; it makes up the fibres of your bones. It is your passion; you can go without eating doing this, you do not care if you get paid for it, it is not a means to an end, but an end that provides a means. When you are in your **work** you almost see the end from the beginning and you work towards that end that you envision. Whereas a job is something you do to keep the bills paid, any month you don't get paid you run a mile because you need to keep things going, it is someone else's vision, you always want a vacation from it, trust me if you are on your **work** you will still do your **work** even on vacation. A simple thing to remember is that your job leaves you *Just Over Broke*. I'm not saying jobs are bad you can have them as a means to sponsor your work, jobs can be temporary bus stops on your journey, but don't be lured to stay longer than you should. They may just retire you with nothing, but a gold wristwatch saying "thank you John" and then you go and wait for death. Have you noticed once people retire it doesn't take long for them to die? Life is an opportunity to fulfil purpose; once you stop working you are telling God 'I might as well die I can't work anymore'. There is more to life than that; make a difference whilst you can.

Note, as a principle; life has a way of rewarding people who followed their true work rather than a job. People who followed their work leave legacies and inheritance for their future generations, but people who follow jobs leave nothing but debts for their children to pay off because people get stuck in the rat race, of which we know that the only price to win in the rat race is that of the bigger rat.

Change things today, leave an inheritance and legacy, not debts or nothing.

Fulfilment comes by fulfilling your why

This to me will help you answer the question 'how do I know what my why is?' We often allow ourselves to get distracted whilst on course to our why. This is because life gets in the way as I have already stated above.

The truth is if you are doing something right now and you do not feel fulfilled doing it, maybe you are studying for a degree that you do not see yourself practising, or you're in a job that you do not derive any fulfilment from; my advice to you is *Leave!!!!!!!* (Plan to exit, when your plan is developed, then exit) You might ask, 'what if I have responsibilities?' I know you do, however, this is also the classic excuse people use sometimes to remain in the same position they have been. They feel bound to their Job, and I understand it is not easy, but I maintain *leave*. Leaving a job won't kill you. At worst, go part-time to allow yourself to make this transition from your job to your work. However, make sure that you've identified your why first; because that is the only way you can withstand the torrent of challenges and questions that will come your way. However, if you have found your why, *literally run for your life!!!!!!!!!!!!!*

It will not be easy, but stick to your why, it will surely pay off, you will be more fulfilled taking small strides towards the fulfilment of your why than making leaps in something you are not passionate about or destined to do.

Management and managers are people who have mastered the techniques of keeping you at their company, you are part of a management report on staff retention which they need to submit to the board of Directors, do not become a victim to their schemes, bonus's, pay rises, promotions, etc. it is all a scheme to keep you there (where you are, broke, in debt, unfulfilled, useless, no legacies, debt inheritance for your kids, retired and waiting for death) *Flee!!!!!!!!!!!!!!!!!!!!*

My Story

I started writing this book roughly at age 13, so I will take you on a brief journey to my life as a 26-year-old man. I'm exactly twice the age I was when I started this book and it makes me weep that so much time has been lost. I've been very selfish in refusing to dedicate sufficient time to get this out to you and I pray God forgives me.

Life has been exciting though, I thank God it hasn't been just doom and gloom, God has been faithful truly from the young boy that started this book as an assignment in school to the man I am right now, it can only be God.

I have always been associated with godly morals from a very young age. I remember most people referred to me as pastor from the young age of seven. As cool as that might sound, it didn't make me one of the popular kids in school. Most times people kept their distance and would only come to me when they wanted to talk about God. Academically I wasn't the best, although I did well in maths and CRK (Christian religious knowledge); I was reliably amongst the bottom of the class. As you can imagine, my parents were not at all happy about how I performed in school, neither were my private tutors who were paid quite significantly to teach me. This trend did not change from primary through to secondary school, but something quite significant during my junior years in secondary school was that my love for God intensified by a huge margin. My Bible was always by my side and luckily, I had friends just like me. This new environment which had me away from home and amid a couple of friends who I felt were like me, energised my passion for the things of God. Due to this, a majority of what I remember from my time in junior secondary was either preaching to schoolmates, singing in every church service, partly leading a daily student fellowship, annoyingly waking up students for their daily devotion and leading this, praying for an average of two hours every day, and praying with the leadership team of the fellowship for upwards of four hours every night; all this whilst I was in school (boarding school). Our Vice Principal once called my parents into a meeting and asked me to leave, but my curious self hovered around his door to listen to their conversation, he said "if academics were to be about the bible your son will be one of our best students, but since we have to cover a variety of subjects, unfortunately, we don't think there is any hope for your son". As you can imagine I didn't have a great trip home that day. Not very long after that period, my family relocated to England. I was so excited, I thought I was stepping into heaven. I remember not minding the heat in Nigeria as I very sanctimoniously suited and booted made my way to the airport. I was sweating profusely, but I did not mind because I thought I dressed suitably for where I was going. The moment I realised that we had touched down at Gatwick airport, I also understood that humans were not the first to create freezers - God was. The cold was immense, to say the least, but I guess with the excitement of seeing my mum after a long while and the jacket that quickly followed I am alive to tell the story.

It wasn't long at all before I realised that the UK offered two sides of the coin very apparently. Within a matter of hours, I started experiencing a totally different culture. Initially, it was very exciting until I started school again. Having no clue how to associate with my new peers, everything was different. I stood out like a sore thumb and this wasn't just an expression, it was a reality. I was the third black in my school at the time and the other two were born here in the UK. The familiarity I was used to back home wasn't received as well here, so my brotherly infectiousness like we did in Africa; let's just say it wasn't appreciated. At times it was well decorated with awkwardness. There were a few ignorant statements by some students. I guess if I knew what bullying was at the time, I might have said I was being bullied; people said unkind words to me and I often enjoyed extra seats on overcrowded school buses and in class. I remember students who asked how I felt living in a house now and wearing nice clothes. Quite frankly I think the reason I didn't react to some of their insults was that sometimes I didn't understand them or let's just say my understanding was sometimes in retrospect. A lot happened to say the least, but I got through it.

It was now the period to take my A-level exams, I remember one of our head of years genuinely advising my parents to send me to learn a trade. He was one hundred percent sure I couldn't get the grades to get into university, I would say my parents certainly believed in me, although looking back, I was enrolled to do plumbing around this same period, but let's call it a coincidence. To the surprise of my teachers, I passed my A Levels. Okay… to be honest after a few trials, but I did it.

I got into university. The first lecture at university "Earth Material": I remember my lecturer; let's call him Mr Shawn for the sake of privacy. So, shortly after Mr Shawn exchanged pleasantries with the whole class he said to us "A relatively high percentage of you will fail this course and some of you will drop out". I quickly started to regret choosing a course I could hardly pronounce. "Engineering geology and geotechnics" it sounded so cool and for once my parents could hold their shoulders high. Their son who they were losing hope in was now surely going to become an Engineer. I was elated by the Idea, I tried, I gave four years of my life trying to prove a point and trying to make my parents proud. Again I failed, it just wasn't working. I remember I bought a DSLR camera towards the end of my A-levels which I used for freelance photography, let's just say: the business was doing relatively well at university, I spent most of my pocket money investing in more camera accessories and fostering a despised less glamorous area of my life which was my love for business. Although I was an engineering student I developed a habit of attending some business school lectures because of a passion I developed for it during my A-levels, this meant that I had a relative grasp of the business subject matter. At this point I was growing a reputation especially amongst the African students as the business engineer; this meant that a lot of business students within my circles came to me for help when they were stuck or overwhelmed with their work. I could easily demystify complicated business issues by providing critically evaluated solutions. On Average, most students who came to me for advice achieved a grade of 2:1 on any work I was consulted. However, in my own engineering related work, I never achieved such a score even with double the effort.

"Have you ever seen water flow up a mountain? Well, neither can you fight against who you really are - a fish only excels in water"

I finally grew the balls I felt I needed to decide my own path. I took a very bold step at this point. I went to the head of department on the MBA course to inquire about what it will take for me to be accepted into her course. She explained a few different paths to the MBA and this included options that did not involve me finishing my engineering degree. I could just call it a day and leave with the qualifications I had achieved so far.

I decided to make the most fearful decision of my life so far; yes, I left my engineering course just a year before I would have graduated. However, my logic was; I didn't want to spend another day doing anything that did not contribute to the future of my dreams.

"My advice to you; be careful when you make a permanent decision based on temporary situations"

I spent quite a while very depressed about life, I was a university dropout and a depraved selfish failure that wouldn't amount to much in life. Those were not necessarily my thoughts but the words of very close people around me. I finally decided after a period of constant bickering with close relatives that I'd had enough. I decided that it was time to move out of my parent's house, without money or a place to go. In a very emotional state a friend of mine who I am eternally grateful to, allowed me to sleep on his couch for a couple of weeks. As you can imagine, this turned to almost a year. At this time, I tried to revive the business I had started before my world started falling apart. I got a meagre job that had me out of the house for 16 hours a day. I actually really enjoyed my job because it afforded me a lot of time to read and to binge on motivational videos and sermons by several great men who I aspired to be like. After several months with my new found inspiration, I took some strides with the business which included obtaining funding so that we could buy much-needed equipment. I thought this was it, I'm now going to become a millionaire very soon. I enrolled in a course that would eventually lead me to an MBA and I felt things were finally coming together. My first purchase was a company van with almost half of the funds. As I drove off after the purchase from a guy who I didn't know, who I met at a location I didn't quite know, I very quickly realised that the van had a significant noise coming from the engine. What I didn't realise at this point though was just how significant this was until I drove to the nearest mechanic who said that the clutch and gearbox were very bad and had to be replaced. I naively said to him please go ahead and fix it. He confidently said to me in response; "it will take about two weeks and it will cost you £2500". Immediately, my joy was turned into mourning.

Quick Lesson before I continue: Please do your due diligence before you make any decision; avoid decisions that are imposed by impulse. Study deals before you take them and always seek counsel.

"Where no counsel is, the people fall: but in the multitude of counsellors there is safety" Proverbs 11:14

Without going into details, my business enterprise was unsuccessful. I ended up losing almost everything. I couldn't complete the payment for the course I had started, and neither could I afford my rent. I felt it was unfair to allow my friend to pay the house rent alone, so I willingly agreed to leave so that he could get a new housemate. I left with all my things and made myself comfortable inside my van. Rock bottom was an understatement for where I found myself, and at this point going home would have been a very humiliating option.

I had literally nothing at this point; food was just bread with water. My bed was the cold seats of my van; shower was a nearby gym which I had a friend's pin code to; heater was a multitude of clothes. I spent most nights crying myself to sleep whilst enduring the fierce cold. I was very furious that God would allow me to go through this horrible period. I was so angry with myself and with everyone I knew who I felt should have looked out for me. One very cold night as I was in my usual sorrowful state, I saw a heap of clothes in the field just in front of me. I approached to investigate further, and I realised this was actually an old woman who I remember helping carry some of her belongings several months ago on her way to the train station. Well, so I thought. It became very apparent that this woman actually slept in an open field and she literally carried all her belongings by hand wherever she went. Tears trickled down my cheeks, as the weight of my challenges suddenly meant nothing. I had a van to sleep in and keep my belongings safe; I had bread to eat, and I could go to the gym to freshen up. I was also very young and could deal with this stress compared to this woman who must have been at least seventy. I felt so ungrateful, I thought I had hit rock bottom, but this encounter made me realise that bottom was in levels and some bottoms made others a very privileged position. This encounter was life-changing. Since that very day, no matter the challenge that arose, it was nothing, because I could now think beyond myself. No matter how bad things are for me in comparison to what others were going through, I discovered that I am often privileged.

Before I continue

I appreciate that you might be faced with quite painful challenges; my advice is to always consider what some people around you are going through. Often, I've found myself grateful rather than depressed whenever I've done this. It helps reduce the weight of the challenge, and a secret I'd love to share is; it helps you come up with solutions once your mind has reduced the gravity of the problem that you were faced with. A friend once told me that if everyone was to truly present the issues facing them and everyone was asked to analyse the issues others faced and pick another person's problem, we will each end up picking ours back up, because although a lot of people act as though everything is ok, people are actually faced with a lot of masked up issues.

For a few more weeks I continued to find shelter in my van. My belief in abandoning everything and burning the bridges to the things that do not align to my future started to develop cracks. Suddenly, I was regretting my decision and stubbornness to follow what I felt was my own path in life. This pressure got to me and I started to retrace my steps. I went back to my engineering lecturer who was hesitant, but allowed me back to engineering school. My parents were happy with me again, and so was the system because they decorated me with a much-needed student finance and maintenance loan which I severely needed. Alas, I could rent a house again. Finally, I understood how the children of Israel felt when they were regretting leaving slavery in the land of Egypt (Numbers 14:2).

I want to let you know that the systems of this world are geared up to make the conformable comfortable. If you are happy to be mediocre everyone will be happy with you. You can't be too happy because they aren't; you can't have a lot of money because they don't; you can't look forward to work because they hate their jobs. Basically, if you want people around you to understand you and be happy with you, then just be average. Be born, go to school, get a job you can't stand, pay tax and bills, marry someone you tolerate, get a house you can barely afford, give birth to kids you have no time for, retire with nothing, die and leave your kids with little to nothing or debts. Unfortunately, as cold as it might sound, what I just described is the life of most people. There's more to life. If this is you right now, I am not trying to condemn you. I know you are trying your hardest, but I just hope you realise you have more to offer. You can achieve a lot more if you can work smarter, rather than harder.

This is however often achieved when you are working in your own path. I believe in you.

As you might have already guessed correctly, I barely lasted in Engineering for one lecture. My first day back reminded me of every reason I left. This time, I didn't bother telling anyone, I literally just stopped attending lectures and I left it for everyone to figure out that I was not interested.

"Don't do this at home"

At this point there was no way back, if people were not initially upset with me, now they were. My lecturers were upset, friends were disappointed, and my parents at this point were losing hope. It was time to really become clear about why I was alive. I had an idea of some things I'd like to have; five to seven nice properties, a very successful business, wife and kids, money that extends help to so many people without diminishing, a few degrees, etc. However, as much as these are valid wants, they're only ambitions, which are very different from *why we are here*.

Your 'why' is a greater force than any other discovery you will make in this life. Until you find it out, you will have a disconnection with everything you attempt to do. I went in search to discover my *why*, I searched in books and the scripture to see if I'd find my *why* in them, just like what was done in Luke 4:17-21 *[17] And there was delivered unto him the book of the prophet Isaiah. And when he had opened the book, he found the place where it was written,*

[18] The Spirit of the Lord is upon me because he hath anointed me to preach the gospel to the poor; he hath sent me to heal the broken-hearted, to preach deliverance to the

captives, and recovering of sight to the blind, to set at liberty them that are bruised,

[19] To preach the acceptable year of the Lord.

[20] And he closed the book, and he gave it again to the minister and sat down. And the eyes of all them that were in the synagogue were fastened on him.

[21] And he began to say unto them, this day is this scripture fulfilled in your ears.

I wanted to discover my *why* inside literature and Gods word. Whilst I found quite generic reasons for being, I knew every Christian had access to them and could claim the same. However, I discovered some patterns. I discovered that everything created was for advancement, preservation, and protection of life. This meant that my purpose must be aligned with these principles in order to be genuine and from God (my creator and manufacturer).

No created thing can ever decide its own function, it is always up to the manufacturer to build certain features and functions into anything they create. If there's ever a malfunction it is also the manufacturer who has the ability to fix what he or she manufactured. This does not mean that other people will not have purported solutions; they just won't have the real deal. This is why a lot of people who have in the past relied on their therapist, gurus, psychiatrist, and some so-called men of God have always found themselves used and worse-off than they started, but this is not to say that you can't find great professionals who can provide a lot of help. My opinion however still remains; God is the only one who has the true solution to any human challenge.

After the discovery of a few guiding principles from the word of God, I was still uncertain about my purpose, but certain I could not be misled about it because whatever it was, it had to align with the will of the Manufacturer. My understanding of my purpose I discovered was hinged to my relationship with God.

The bible says we should *"ask, and we shall receive, seek and we shall find, knock and the door will be opened unto us" Matthew 7:7.* Knowledge of what to do when faced with a circumstance is far more important than knowing how to do it. I had discovered from the study of God's word that who we are, is innate *"Before I formed you in the womb I knew you, before you were born I set you apart; I appointed you as a prophet to the nations." Jeremiah 1:5.*

So if I lacked knowledge of something that is already in me, the best solution is to seek for it. If I asked others for it, no one would know. If I knocked on people's doors for it, I'd probably be turned away. Hence all the disappointments I had received up until this point in my life.

Some Keys that Helped Me Find Me

Prayer, because I do not trust myself to know me, but I trust God who made me

"Trust in the Lord with all your heart, and lean not in your own understanding; in all your ways acknowledge him and he shall direct your path" Proverbs 3: 5-6. The creator is best placed to know about the created. God knows me a lot more than I can ever get to know myself, every characteristic; likes and dislikes, temperament or perks I have. God knows why he placed it in me, and He also knows the best ways for me to harness the strengths within my character; therefore who better to trust to direct me in the discovery of my purpose in life.

Whatever I can't do for free and be happy I shouldn't do at all

A lot of us are frustrated every day we wake up because we know that the job we are pretty much stuck with or the courses we are studying have nothing to do with the future we envision. Most of us feel imprisoned by our current situation and this keeps us in a cycle of stunted growth if any growth at all. Until you close some doors that are currently open in your life, you'd never be able to see or even attempt to open other doors accessible to you. It is not every opportunity that is your opportunity, be very mindful. I have found from my life so far that *my biggest distractions were not necessarily the obvious bad choices, but the 'good' choices that were not right for me.*

There are some licences that you need to let expire, there are some jobs you need to walk away from, some friends you need spend less time with; if you are the wisest amongst your friends you need some new ones. There are things that you need to time-box (things that must not exceed a time). I discovered the things that were natural to me also allowed me the opportunity to flourish: we can also see this law apply in nature. There are some plants that do not grow in certain environments, but when placed in their right environment they flourish.

Any place my gifts do not flourish, I must stay away

Just as I pointed out above, everything created has an ideal environment, and according to the principles I found in Genesis 1 & 2, the environment always preceded the occupant. Seas were created before fish, light and soil preceded plants; and plants did not grow until man was created to till the soil. So rain waited for man to be created before the full compose of plant life aggregated, Genesis 2:5. God does not waste his resources, He told his disciples *"wherever you are not welcomed, dust your feet and leave, find someone worthy and abode there"*, Matthew 10:14. This principle is very important because the more you spend time in the wrong place, the less time you have for your right place, get-up and leave. Just to clarify, I'm not talking about your marriage here, but if you still have one minute before you say I do, you are better off leaving than spending your life in misery. Anyone who cannot add to you during courtship will remove from you during marriage. According to the principles I saw in God's word, whatever keeps you where you were yesterday actually takes away from you. There is really no life in stagnation. The fact that you are still where you were yesterday means that you are worse off than you were yesterday (Matthew 25:14-30, Matthew 21: 18-46). Set goals for yourself and seek to actively improve yourself daily.

If you place a seed on your kitchen marble worktop for 40 years nothing will grow, place that same seed in the right soil come back in 40 years you might have a forest.

Dr Myles Munroe

Identify my strengths and amplify them, my weaknesses were to get the least of my attention

I remember reading the story of the talents in Matthew 25: 14-30 and feeling sorry that the person who had the most was added to whilst the person who had the least, had it taken from him. Feeling sorry for him, that's me being human, but I have discovered that nature works via principle irrespective of our personal opinions. If you have nothing in your bank account after a while your bank might close your account, but if you have something they add interest to it. If you wanted a loan for a business or house, the guy who had money will get a lot more, the one who doesn't have any will get none "unfortunately". Everyone is clearly adopting God's principles to succeed. I have been within the business environment for a while now, and businesses that did not apply God's principles have failed and are failing woefully. Lionel Messi is important if you have a football team, but if we saw him in a surgeons outfit about to perform surgery on a loved one, we'd all be alarmed, not because Lionel Messi isn't good at something, but because we know he's good at football, not surgery. A cheetah has no competition when it comes to being the fastest land animal, but if a cheetah went for a flying competition, even a chicken will defeat the cheetah. Spend time developing the area you are good at. Success is easier and less strenuous when you are in your own area. Hence, the principle of God says *Let every man mind his own business.*

(1 Thessalonians 4:11)

Pay my mind before I pay my debts

This might be controversial, but then again, it's a principle that works. The content of a thing determines the value of it. *As a man thinks in his heart so is he* (Proverbs 23:7); *Wisdom is the principal thing and with all you're getting get understanding.* (Proverbs 4:7). Your mind is key to everything (Proverbs 8:10-11, Job 28:15, Psalms 119:72). Therefore, before your resources are expended to anything else, make sure your mind has also been fed. One of the ways I know quality people is the repository of their library. I've never asked great men I've come across for money, I've always asked for books. If they couldn't give it to me, I ask for recommendations and I buy it for myself. *"The lamp of the body is the eye. If therefore your eye is good, your whole body will be full of light. ^{23} But if your eye is bad, your whole body will be full of darkness. If therefore the light that is in you is darkness, how great is that darkness"* (Matthew 6:22-23).

Pay your mind and your debts will be taken care of, pay your debts first and you're still where you were.

Relationship with me prioritised over relationships with others

A lot of us look for people to stay around because we cannot stand our own company. If you are so boring that you cannot stand yourself why should others stand you? Apart from my relationship with God, the main relationship that matters is my relationship with me. Until I get to know me I am of no value to someone else. In fact, if you don't know yourself you're a burden to others. Notice in Genesis, God created a single human first? Adam was already running with the purpose of God for his life before God decided to make a companion (fit, aligned) for Adam. Until you know yourself, you do not have the ability to know the value of those around you. You will make a much better friend to others if you know yourself. Companionship or relationship should occur only after you have fully identified who you are. My next point is very vital for guys. Work was given to Adam, long before Eve. Work before woman. For the ladies, if a guy does not know his work, forget his money and muscles, they're completely useless to you. As a matter of fact, the muscle will be used to muzzle you. Notice I used the word "work" (what you are created to do) not "job" (What you are paid to do that you won't do except you are paid). An individual can have a "job" and not have "work". You need to absorb this to avoid loads of mistakes that await people who do not align with this principle.

Problems I see are invitations to solutions I have

A good mechanic listens to the engine of a car and diagnoses its problem. A dentist is forever checking the teeth of everyone around them. An evangelist sees the most depraved areas as ripe missionary fields. *Sometimes the problems we have the opportunity to detect are indications of the problems we have the capacity to solve.*

The people whose pain I feel and whose ignorance I despise, I'm called to teach

I have a huge heart for people who have been imprisoned by their minds. I feel the pain of blacks in the western world trying to make something out of their life. I feel the pain of their ignorance on ways they could come out of penury. I feel the pain of the businessman who does not see a way forward. I feel the pain of a human who has given up on life and does not know a way to hope. Those are some of the areas that get me crying sometimes, but also those are the candidates for the message of hope that God packaged in every fibre of my being. What are yours?

The qualities I admired in the men/women I looked up to were a mirror to the qualities that are yet to be amplified in me

What qualities do you admire in me or any other person you look up to? Write it down below

1. _____
2. _____
3. _____
4. _____
5. _____
6. _____
7. _____
8. _____
9. _____
10._____

(Reflect on this)

What if I told you this is who you are, but you still haven't developed yourself appropriately in those areas. This is true because we see in others a mirror of who we are.

Being unafraid to shut the door to areas that are not growing and focusing on that which is

I have dealt with this earlier, but it's here again for emphasis. The longer time you spend with the wrong thing, the shorter time you'd have for the right thing.

God pasturing over men pastors

I'm sorry pastors, the Bible says *"The Lord is my shepherd; I shall not want"* Psalms 23:1, your roles are important if you point people to God. You ought to encourage people to study God's word more than you encourage them to listen to you preach. The bible says *"God's word is a lamp unto our paths and a light unto our feet"* Psalms 119:105. A lot of people have gone astray because they've listened to their pastor on what to do, who to marry, etc. The reason that is sure to fail is because God never intended to be replaced by any man.

Therefore, your pastor has no capacity to be God in your life. Any Pastor not directing you to the word of God is directing you to your doom, not every word from a man of God is sanctioned by God, therefore it is your responsibility to question and verify every word from a man or woman of God through God's Word. Any pastor who you can't question, you ought to be careful to ensure he/she is from God. Having a relationship with God is not for lazy people, it is for people who are determined not to remain in ignorance. You have to study God's word for yourself. That is the key to finding direction in life.

Books before food

This is very simple, but a principle to find direction in life; look at Job *"I have not departed from the commandment of His lips; I have treasured the words of His mouth more than my necessary food"* Job 23:12, Jesus also said *"Man shall not live by bread alone, but by every word that proceeds out of the mouth of God"* Matthew 4:4. Food is necessary for your body, but books that are enlightening are necessary for your mind and future.

Good food flushes down a toilet, good books flourish your future.

Distinguishing between why I was born and how I was to fulfil my why

A problem births a solution. Some of us have solutions but we do not know the problems they solve. That's a nuisance. However, in the right environment, it becomes a solution. You might have a voice, but if there is no substance attached to what you say, you are called a noisemaker; but if you have content inside of you and you seek for a way to express it, then your voice or music is a good "*how*" or means of expression.

So your content is your "why" and your talent is a clue to your how.

Sustainability over miracle expectation

This is simply that statement we all know, "**give** a man a **fish** and you feed him for a day; **teach** a man to **fish** and you feed him for a lifetime". Don't pray for my miracle, teach me something that will mean I perform that miracle every day. A lot of people are praying for something within their reach. Some people's hands have never found anything to do and yet they expect God's blessings. Well, the Bible says God will bless the works of your hands (Deuteronomy 28:12, Psalms 90:17), the manual also says, *"A diligent man will stand before Kings and not mean men"* Proverbs 22:29. You've got to *"watch and pray"* Matthew 26:41, notice watch (work) came before prayer, meaning before you say, "God bless me", make sure you have something He can bless you through.

Distinguishing between job and work

"Work" (what you are created to do), "job" (What you are paid to do that you won't do except you are paid).

Creativity over adopting

Uniqueness does not mean buying Gucci whilst others buy Zara, it means that you can go ahead and wear your Gucci and Zara, whilst I am happy to also create my "Mobu clothing line" and rock my own stuff. What I just said is not literal in its form, but it is also: always seek the opportunity to create; everything you see around you today was once an idea on someone's mind.

Standing out over fitting in

Dr Myles Munroe said in his book "Maximising Your Potential" that *"mediocrity has caused those who do a little bit extra to become genius"*. Whilst everyone is busy fitting in, please be okay to stick out. You are special, that doesn't detract from the fact that people around you are also special. It just means that you know yourself. You have a unique **"destiny"** be cool in your own skin. You must not follow the trend, it stops you from setting the trend. Just make sure it preserves, protects, and advances human life, and most importantly that God is glorified through you.

Destiny as a mnemonic

D - Destiny must be **discovered**

E - Destiny must be **equipped**

S – Destiny must have **strategy** backing it up

T – Destiny does **tarry** (You have to persevere)

I – Destiny requires an **investment**

N – Destiny must be in your **niche** (speciality or difference)

Y – Destiny must **yield** (This is in two-fold; your destiny must be yielded to God and your destiny must yield fruits "products" that can be reproduced).

What is Purpose, Mission, and Vision

Purpose

When an issue (problem, need) is raised, purpose is a very high-level requirement or solution for it. Purpose identifies an intention to provide a solution to an issue. In project management, we might sometimes refer to this as an *"epic"*. For example, let's use the scenario of the first set of humans on earth who we might assume were living in open fields, in the forest, or around mountains. Wherever these first set of humans might have found themselves, a common theme was that they were exposed to cold, rain, snow, deadly, animals, etc. After a while they came together and agreed that something had to be done for them to have shelter from the elements, this more or less becomes their purpose. ***Like the first set of humans,*** **we want** *shelter* ***so that*** *we can be protected from the elements and reduce death amongst us.*

This is an epic in project management and by that virtue, it needs to be broken down a lot more, but in this context, this is their purpose.

> *"Your purpose is your why"*

Mission

Continuing with the same scenario, place yourself in the shoes of the first set of humans who had no clue about anything that provided shelter from the elements. If you were given the purpose above, in all honesty even as an experienced project management professional, I would not have a clue about what to do to achieve such a huge task. Which is why a mission is important because it provides a level of direction to help achieve the purpose. I can imagine these first men and women coming together to evaluate options available to them, they might have had the options of a tree house, a cave, a mud house, a thatched house, a shed, a bungalow, a mansion, or a skyscraper. However, after extensive evaluation, let's assume they chose a mud house because of the resources available to them at the time. This invariably reduces their option and sets their direction on a particular mission. Their mission will be **as a human I will like to** *build mud houses*

so that *we can be protected from the elements and reduce deaths amongst us.* As much as I would agree with my fellow project management professionals that this is not quite detailed enough to be called a *user story* (A broken down epic or purpose), but in this context, I will call this a *user story*. If given this, I am sure you will agree with me that you know a bit more about your purpose to understand at least which options to eliminate. However, we can all still agree that you do not have enough details yet about how to build your mud house, how many rooms it will contain, where the doors will be, or if it would need a window. I am sure you can add so many other things to this list, and this leads me to the next point on "vision".

"Your mission is your what"

Vision

'The architectural components that make up one's purpose or put simply 'purpose in pictures'. This is a detailed project plan. It is the project output of an architect. It deals with all the details of how the mission is going to be achieved. It is at this point in our scenario that we eliminate any confusion, we get to know how the mud house will look, number of rooms, windows, doors, decor, fittings, etc. It is visual, it is well researched, and it must be written (*"write a vision and make it plain on tablets, that he may run who reads it"* Habakkuk 2:2) or drawn out so that whoever sees it can easily understand what the purpose is trying to achieve and how it is going to solve the problem for which it was initiated. It is a prototype. The bible says, *"Where there is no vision, the people perish" Proverbs 29:18.* Like the point we made when we defined mission; mission eliminates the wrong options and sets you on a course, but mission does not tell you how to do what it wants you to do. Vision, however, goes into those details and really expatiates on how it wants you to go about achieving the mission and purpose for which you have set out.

Examples:

- As a human we will like a door at the front of the house so that we can easily enter and exit the house

- As a human we will like a window so that air can easily circulate

- As a human we will like a roof so that we can be protected from snow, rain, and excessive sunlight

- As a human we will like a fire place so that we can warm ourselves when it is cold.

"Your vision is your how"

Components of Your Why

Discovery

Your why is not known; it is discovered and continually uncovered.

You must find what makes you unique. The most important thing in this life is not life itself; it is the day you find out why you are living. What problem are you born to solve? Everything created is a solution to a problem. The fact that you are living is proof that you still have something to offer; someone somewhere is relying on you for the solution to their problem. The only thing that authorizes you for a position of influence and wealth is the problem you are destined to solve. It makes you outstanding in a crowd; it is the passkey to everything you've ever desired. Men will flock to you, happily parting ways with their hard-earned money just for you to solve that problem for them. You are sitting on a gold mine whilst trading your time for money; if you learn how to spend money to buy back your time, then you are onto something really good. Most of you are physically ill because so far you have not discovered your why. The reason you feel unfulfilled in your JOB (just over broke), unhappy with your life, and very inadequate in class, is simply because you have not discovered and uncovered your why. Discover your why and start living.

Enhancement/development

Preparation is more important than presentation. After the discovery of your purpose, you must take the responsibility of developing your area of specialization, it is a competition out there, but your conviction of purpose can make a way for you, however, you need a strength of character to keep you there and this must be consistently developed.

Provision

Pro- Professional/ specialist

Vision- Architectural components of a purpose. Insight into the future.

Provision means providing professional/specialist insight, solution or component in your area of vision birth by a purpose.

The only reason you might be providing sub-standard products or irrelevant services to your clients or employers is simply because you are not providing what you are destined to provide. Like I said earlier we would all love Lionel Messi in our football team, but not as our surgeon. Perhaps you are suffering from this issue, but trying your hardest to do something you are not destined to do, will make your efforts futile. If you find your area, develop it, and provide it to the world, then watch and see who you emerge into in a few years to come.

Conclusion

It was the accumulation of all the above that I harnessed to discover my why; I pray it helps you also.

After searching and trying to put the pieces of my life together I could see the light because some patterns started to become highlighted to me, about me. One of the key things was that some of the things I loved were instantly eliminated from a why, to a means or a how. That is; my love for music was no longer a why, music became and now is a means through which I communicate a particular message. My love for writing or speaking or blogging or vlogging is not a why, but God gave me those tools because he knew that He had a message I had to deliver to His people. My natural inclination towards leadership, politics, business, and purpose were not my callings, but my God-given areas of influence. My general disposition to being told "you can't", inferiority, and mediocrity; were no signs of pride, but anger towards limitations, barriers, and subjugation. Now all these I knew already about myself, but never did it occur to me that my purpose was hinged to these. A lot of people called it stubbornness, infatuation, pride, and fantasy living, but on a particular day while fasting, praying and meditating as I walked from 'The Hard' in Portsmouth towards the Business school, I heard a gentle voice say, "You're called to provide independence to people's barriers". That was all I needed for that time. Joy and peace engulfed me at that moment because I knew it was a matter of time for God to fully unveil what my purpose on earth was and how I must go about fulfilling it. With time through a journey of self-exposition, I have found out that my life is all about *providing independence to people's barriers* (my why) *by imparting knowledge in the areas of leadership, purpose and business* (my what), *through the medium/media of music, writing, philanthropy, and public speaking* (some aspects of my how). This clearly means that my natural flair and interest in all of the above was never a coincidence, but a God-incidence. Since I made this discovery no devil or Angel has been able to convince me otherwise, no new trend will trade in my life, all my vigour and resources have been channelled towards fulfilling my God-given assignment, and Yes, I am happier with my life. Every day is great because I know the reason for that day, unlike before.

So, what is it that I do now, you might ask? Presently, apart from writing books like this one, I also compose and write songs. I'm still on the path to pursuing my MBA; I have completed a post-grad in strategic management and leadership. I work as a management consultant, business analyst and project manager. I'm also an investor, public speaker, and business coach. In the area of philanthropy; I just started an initiative that will help sponsor some less-privileged kids through school, I am starting with just four students for now, but this is a small step towards a leadership institute that will cater for no less than a thousand individuals in the future completely free. As you can probably imagine, the future does hold a lot of prospects. I am so excited to see what God has in stock; especially with the various projects He has placed on my mind to impact this generation and future ones.

Trust me everything good about me right now started when I began to work within God's purpose for my life; unexpected resources and favour came through various channels to enable me to work in my purpose and fulfil my God-given visions, which reminds me of Genesis 2:5 *"Now no shrub had yet appeared on the earth and no plant had yet sprung up, for the LORD God had not sent rain on the earth and there was no one to work the ground"*. Perhaps for you also, resources might be waiting at the place of your obedience.

*"Many are the plans in a person's heart,
but it is the LORD's purpose that prevails"*

Proverbs 19:21

In simpler terms; you might have a lot of plans for yourself, but God will only foot the bill for those plans which are His.

For you, I pray this book sheds light that directs you back to God; I pray that the fullness of your purpose will be unveiled through this encounter; and finally, I pray that your impact and influence will be heard all over the world, and God will receive all the glory for your life. Amen

One more thing left very important!

Oh, One More Thing

If you've never been exposed to this knowledge in the past and will love to give your life to this God who changed my life and who will truly unveil your true potential for free. The One, who made you, knows you, loves you and paid the ultimate sacrifice to free you from the bonds of sin and death. I employ you to read out the prayer below to begin this journey to the unending breakthroughs in life; Read this aloud

"Father, I know that I have broken your laws and my sins have separated me from you. I am truly sorry, and now I want to turn away from my past sinful life toward you. Please forgive me, I believe that Your Son, Jesus Christ died for my sins, and was resurrected from the dead, is alive, and can hear my prayer. I invite Jesus to become the Lord of my life, to rule and reign in my heart from this day forward. Please send your Holy Spirit to help me obey You, and to do Your will for the rest of my life. In Jesus' name, I pray, Amen."

Dear friend, you've just made the most important decision of your life, I'm sure you won't regret it. In fact, I guarantee that from this day forward you will see your life moving in the right direction. I urge you to find a local Bible-believing church where you will meet others who are on the same path as you, and where your faith can be nurtured to great heights. Remain blessed.

Summary

You owe it to this world not to die with your vision; the cemeteries already have stolen a lot from us

- Dare to dream outside your confines; you are the only one who can stop yourself from fulfilling your dreams. Nothing is impossible to him that believes
- Have you ever seen water flow up a mountain? Well, neither can you fight against who you really are - a fish only excels in water
- The biggest distractions are not necessarily the obvious bad choices, but the 'good' choices that are not right for me
- You can achieve a lot more if you can work smarter, rather than harder
- Whatever keeps you where you were yesterday actually takes away from you, the fact that you are still where you were yesterday means that you are worse off than you were yesterday

- Good food flushes down a toilet, good books flourish your future
- Pay your mind and your debts will be taken care of, pay your debts first and you're still where you were
- The problems we have the opportunity to detect are an indication of the problem we have the capacity to solve
- Knowledge of what to do when faced with a circumstance is far more important than knowing how to do it
- Your content is your "why" and your talent is a clue to your how
- Following the trend, can stop you from setting the trend

Notes

Notes

Another book by the Author

African Future Leaders: What the Next Generation of African Leaders Need to Build a Successful African Society

If you've ever wondered why Africa and Africans (People of African origin) seem to be left behind when it comes to global development, especially when you consider socio-economic factors that expedite economic growth, global positioning and a strong sense of identity, then wonder no more; this book is an exposé into the African mind and consciousness, it journeys from the origin of the African to the present realities that Africans are faced with. You will learn how to discover your true identity, develop your gifts and provide your unique leadership to the present and future generations.

Grab a copy today from most online retail stores.

www.ingramcontent.com/pod-product-compliance
Lightning Source LLC
Chambersburg PA
CBHW052331220526
45472CB00001B/377